My Funny V

This book is from ....Emma Clifford....

to my Valentine ....Richard....

who ☐ is quite good-looking -- on a cloudy
        day

who ☑ has a face like a million dollars,
        all green and wrinkled

who ☐ reminds me of gooseberry fool; sickly

who ☐ is just like a peach, with a heart of
        stone

Other books from Methuen Teens

KATIE WALES
My Funny Valentine

Illustrated by Paul Dowling

Methuen

First published as a Methuen Teens paperback original 1988
by Methuen Children's Books Ltd
11 New Fetter Lane, London EC4P 4EE
Text copyright © 1988 Katie Wales
Illustrations copyright © 1988 Paul Dowling
Printed in Great Britain

ISBN 0 416 08452 4

ST VALENTINE'S DAY

No one really knows why February 14th is named after St Valentine. We don't even really know who St Valentine was, because there was more than one saint with that name. Legend has it that one Valentine was imprisoned by the Romans in the fifth century AD for being a Christian, and was sentenced to death. He cured the gaoler's daughter of blindness, but that didn't make any difference to the Romans. He sent her a note before he was executed (on February 14th) saying 'From your Valentine'.

It so happened that February 14th and 15th were holidays for the Romans – the feast of Juno, the queen of the gods, and of Lupercus, their god of fertility. So the Roman feasts and the Christian story were put together, and February 14th became connected with people in love. Legend also says that February 14th is the date when the birds choose their mates.

Lovers have been sending each other presents and flowers on St Valentine's Day since the Middle Ages, but it was the Victorians who started sending greetings cards.

Lots of superstitions and customs have grown up around the idea of courtship, love and St Valentine's Day. Here are just a few examples:

Violets mean faithfulness, but daisies would be bad luck.

It is good luck to be woken up by a kiss on St Valentine's Day and the first person you see will be your Valentine.

Put some sweet flowers under your pillow the night before and you are bound to see your future partner in your dreams . . .

If you see a robin on St Valentine's Day, you will marry a sailor; if you see a sparrow, you will marry a farmer . . .

VALENTINE VERSES

Roses are red,
Violets are blue,
Sugar is sweet,
And so are you . . .

And so are they
That send you this,
And when we meet
We'll have a kiss.

Roses are red,
Violets are blue,
But who needs flowers
When I've got you?

Roses are red,
Violets are blue,
Sugar is sweet,
So why aren't you?

Roses are red,
Violets are blue,
Sugar is sweet –
And I hate you too!

Roses are red,
Violets are blue,
I copied your exams,
And I failed too!

Roses are red,
Violets are blue,
Sugar is sweet,
And expensive too.

Roses are sweet,
Violets too,
So what was left out
When they made you?

Postman, Postman, do your duty,
Take this to my lovely beauty.

Postman, Postman, don't delay,
Do the rhumba all the way.

Postman, Postman, hurry far,
If _____'s not in, then give it to her Ma.

Postman, Postman, haste away
To _____ without delay;
Miss _____ _____ there you'll find,
A nymph that's generous, true and kind.
You'll ramble far to find a better,
So knock in haste, and leave this letter.

Postman, Postman, don't be slow,
Be like Elvis; go, man, go!

CABBAGE
My love is like a brassica

My love is like a cabbage
Divided into two,
The leaves I give to others,
But the heart I give to you.

My pen is black,
My ink is pale,
My love for you
Shall never fail.

_____ _____ is her name,
Single is her station.
Can I be the little man
To make the alteration?

Plenty of love
Tons of kisses,
Hope some day
To be your Mrs.

I would wash all the dishes,
If you'd let me be your Mrs.

Eight o'clock bells are ringing,
Mother, may I go out?
My young man's a-waiting
For to take me out.

First he bought me apples,
Then he bought me pears,
Then he gave me sixpence
To kiss him on the stairs.

Good morrow to you, Valentine!
Curl your locks as I do mine;
Two before and two behind,
Good morrow to you, Valentine.

Peep, fool, peep,
What do you think to see?
Everyone has a Valentine,
And here's one for thee!

The rain makes all things beautiful,
The flowers and grasses, too.
If rain makes all things beautiful,
Why doesn't it rain on you?

Tomorrow is Saint Valentine's Day,
All in the morning betime,
And I a maid at your window,
To be your Valentine.

Good Valentine, be kind to me,
In dreams let me my true love see.

'Twas in a café first they met,
Romeo and Juliet.
And there they first ran into debt,
For Romeo'd what Juliet . . .

I love you, I love you,
Please be my Valentine,
And give me your bubble gum,
Because you're sitting on mine.

THE LANGUAGE OF LOVE . . .

Stuck on what to call your Valentine? Try one of the following names! They've all appeared in the newspapers on St Valentine's Day . . .

Captain Braindeath
Giant Tortoise
Aardvark
Manure
Bags
Ginger-nut
Microwave Kid
Ratty
Snore Baby
Tiger-mate
Beanie
Big Sausage
Chubby Chops
Buzz Buzz
Jelly-head
Old Crusty Eyes
Nose-bag
Pimples
Sea Elephant
Arctic Mammal
Chedge
Golden Swallow
Megastrop
Poody
Scheherazade
Sunny
Yogi

Angel-puss

Babycakes

Chirrup-Chirrup

Gribble

Mini-Mog

Pooh Bear

Schnips

Sweepie

Wuggles

Stupid Monkey

Puffin Pie

Pod Face

Looby Loo

Fuzzypeg

Bunny Wunny

Baggy

Chocolate Brains

Gumboots

Mumpkins

Poopie

Scribble Face

Tea-bags

Woodpigeon

Bagpuss

Crinkle Face

Hairy Hogg

Mutley

Pootle

Scrumbles

Teasel Tendrill

Wiggy Wiggy

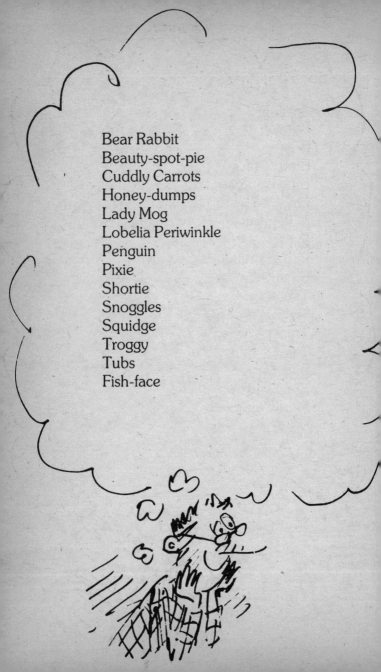

Bear Rabbit
Beauty-spot-pie
Cuddly Carrots
Honey-dumps
Lady Mog
Lobelia Periwinkle
Penguin
Pixie
Shortie
Snoggles
Squidge
Troggy
Tubs
Fish-face

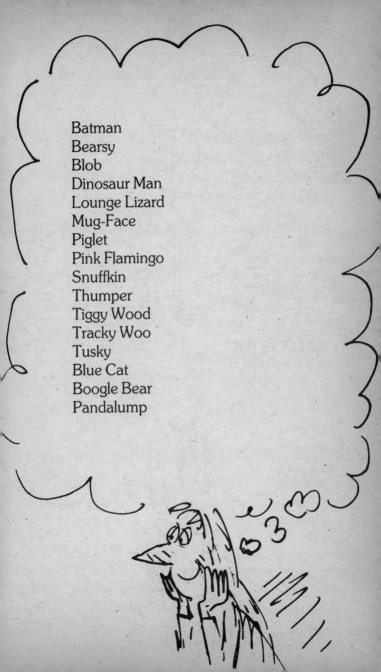

Batman
Bearsy
Blob
Dinosaur Man
Lounge Lizard
Mug-Face
Piglet
Pink Flamingo
Snuffkin
Thumper
Tiggy Wood
Tracky Woo
Tusky
Blue Cat
Boogle Bear
Pandalump

Dogbreath
Fat Cow
Fatty Trollop
Floozie
Green-eyed Dragon
Jelly Belly
Pig Face

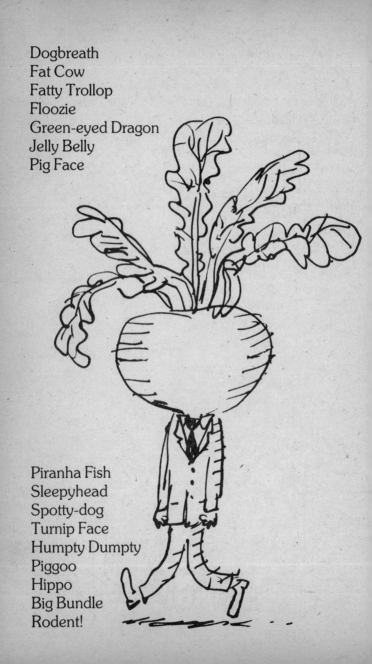

Piranha Fish
Sleepyhead
Spotty-dog
Turnip Face
Humpty Dumpty
Piggoo
Hippo
Big Bundle
Rodent!

VALENTINE GREETINGS

Knock, knock.
Who's there?
Howard.
Howard who?
Howard you like to be my Valentine . . .?

Knock, knock.
Who's there?
Avon.
Avon who?
Avon to be your Valentine.

Knock, knock.
Who's there?
Willy.
Willy who?
Willy still love me tomorrow?

Knock, knock.
Who's there?
Sheila.
Sheila who?
Sheiloves me, sheiloves me not . . .

Knock, knock.
Who's there?
Will.
Will who?
Will you come out with me tonight?

Knock, knock.
Who's there?
Don Juan.
Don Juan who?
Don Juan to see me again?

Knock, knock.
Who's there?
William.
William who?
William marry me?

Knock, knock.
Who's there?
Olive.
Olive who?
I love you too, honey.

Knock, knock.
Who's there?
Aladdin.
Aladdin who?
Aladdin the street is waiting for you . . .

Knock, knock?
Who's there?
Arthur.
Arthur who?
Arthur any more at home like you?

Q. What did the candle say to the match?
A. *You light up my life.*

Q. What did one candle say to another?
A. *Let's go out together.*

Q. What did the light bulb say to the switch?
A. *You turn me on.*

Q. What did one traffic light say to another?
A. *Don't look now, I'm changing.*

Q. What did the letter say to the stamp?
A. *You send me.*

Q. What did the envelope say to the stamp?
A. *Stick with me and we'll go places!*

Q. What did the stamp say to the envelope?
A. *I'm stuck on you.*

Q. What did the pen say to the paper?
A. *I dot my eyes on you.*

Q. What did the glue say to the paper?
A. *Let's stick together.*

Q. What did the librarian say to the book?

A. *Can I take you out?*

Q. What did one squirrel say to another?
A. *I'm nuts about you.*

Q. What was the reply?
A. *You're nuts so bad yourself.*

Q. What did one pig say to another?
A. *I'll give you lots of hogs and kisses.*

Q. What did the bull say to the cow?
A. *When I fall in love, it will be for heifer.*

Q. What did the python say to his girlfriend?
A. *I've got a crush on you.*

Q. What did one shy pebble say to another?
A. *I wish I were a little boulder.*

Q. What did one volcano say to another?
A. *Do you lava me as much as I lava you?*

Q. What did one bell say to another?
A. *Give me a ring some time.*

Q. What did one tiger say to another?
A. *I'm wild about you.*

Q. What did the ram say to his girlfriend?
A. *I love ewe.*

Q. What did the tom-cat say to the tabby-cat?
A. *You're just purr-fect!*

Q. What did the duck say to the drake?
A. *I'm quackers about you.*

Q. What did the flower say to the bee?
A. *I'm sweet on you.*

Q. What did one battery say to another?
A. *I get a big charge out of you.*

Q. What did the electric plug say to the wall?
A. *Socket to me!*

Q. What did the girlfriend say to her ex-
   boyfriend?
A. *I've heard of dream-boats – you're a
   shipwreck!*

Q. What did the stereo needle say to the record?
A. *Would you like to go for a spin?*

Q. What did the robot say to his girlfriend?
A. *I love you watts and watts.*

Q. What did she say?
A. *You're so electrocute.*

Q. What did the magnet say to the pin?
A. *I find you very attractive.*

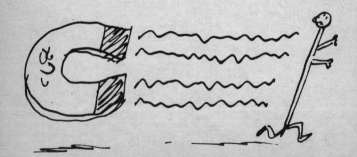

Q. What did one star say to another?
A. *Can you come out tonight?*

Q. What did one shooting-star say to another?
A. *Pleased to meteor.*

Q. What did one calendar say to another?
A. *I have more dates than you.*

Q. What did one fir tree say to another?
A. *Yew the one for me.*

Q. What was the reply?
A. *Tree-mendous – I'm pining for you.*

Q. What did the beaver say to the tree?
A. *It's been nice gnawing you.*

Q. What did one tree say to another?
A. *Don't leaf me alone like this.*

Q. What did Dracula say to his girlfriend?
A. *Are you loathsome tonight?*

Q. What else?
A. *Hi, gore-juice!*

Q. What did Dracula say when he kissed his
   girlfriend goodbye?
A. *Fangs for the memory.*

Q. What did one vampire say to another?
A. *I like your blood type.*

Q. What else?
A. *I'm bats about you.*

Q. What did the vampire say to his sweetheart?
A. *Will you be my ghoulfriend?*

Q. What did Frankenstein's monster say to his girlfriend?
A. *I believe in love at first fright.*

Q. What did one zombie say to another?
A. *You really kill me.*

Q. What did one bat say to another?
A. *Let's hang around together.*

Q. What did one spirit say to another?
A. *You don't stand the ghost of a chance with me.*

Q. What did one mummy say to another?
A. BC-*ing you.*

Q. What did the Invisible Man say to the Invisible Woman?
A. *It's nice not to see you again.*

Q. What did one demon say to another?
A. *Demons are a ghoul's best friend.*

Q. What did one monster say to another?
A. *Beware my ghoulish heart.*

Q. What did the demon say about her
boyfriend?
A. *We're just good fiends.*

Q. What did one witch say to another?
A. *Hallo e'en.*

Q. What did the Eskimo say when he kissed his girlfriend goodbye?
A. *Whalemeat again, don't know where, don't know when . . .*

Q. What did one octopus say to another?
A. *I wanna hold your your hand, hand, hand, hand, hand, hand, hand, hand . . .*

Q. What did one caterpillar say to another?
A. *What a lovely pair of legs, pair of legs, pair of legs . . . .*

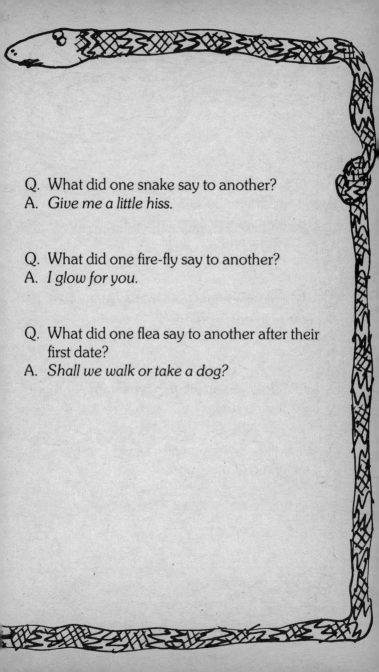

Q. What did one snake say to another?
A. *Give me a little hiss.*

Q. What did one fire-fly say to another?
A. *I glow for you.*

Q. What did one flea say to another after their first date?
A. *Shall we walk or take a dog?*

Q. What did the fish say to the fisherman?
A. *Drop me a line some-time.*

Q. What did the lettuce say to the caterpillar?
A. *You're in my heart.*

Q. What do owls say when it is raining?
A. *Too-wet-to-woo.*

Q. What did one glow-worm say to another?
A. *De-lighted to meet you.*

Q. What did one watch say to another?
A. *Keep your hands to yourself.*

Q. What did the big clock hand say to the little hand?
A. *Don't worry, I'll be back in an hour.*

Q. What else?
A. *Meet me at noon for lunch.*

Q. What did one watch say to another?
A. *Hour you doing?*

Q. What did one accordian say to another?
A. *Every time I squeeze you, I hear music.*

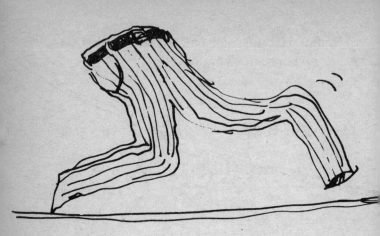

Q. What did the shirt say to the trousers?
A. *Meet me at the clothes-line. That's where*
   I hang out.

Q. What did the lunatic say to his girlfriend?
A. *I'm crazy about you.*

Q. What did one hair say to another hair?
A. *Don't you dare tangle with me!*

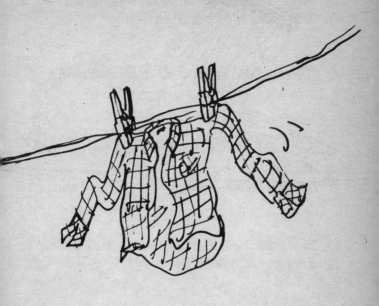

Q. What did the maiden say to St George?
A. *Don't just stand there – slay something.*

Q. What did one tonsil say to the other?
A. *Get dressed – we're being taken out tonight.*

Q. What did the toothpaste say to the
   toothbrush?
A. *Squeeze my bottom and I'll meet you
   outside the tube.*

Q. What did one jelly-baby say to another?
A. *You make my knees turn to jelly.*

Q. What did the butcher say to his girlfriend?
A. *When shall we meat again?*

Q. What did one windscreen wiper say to another?
A. *Isn't it a shame we only meet when it rains.*

Q. What did the hamburger say to the tomato?
A. *That's enough of your sauce!*

Q. What did one banana say to another?
A. *You have lots of appeal.*

Q. What did the gorilla say to his girlfriend?
A. *You drive me bananas.*

Q. What did the calculator say to the
   mathematician?
A. *You can count on me.*

Q. What did the balloon say to the pin?
A. *Hello, Buster!*

Q. What did the boy say to his girlfriend?
A. *You look like a famous film-star – Lassie!*

Q. What else?
A. *You look like an Italian dish – spaghetti.*

Q. What else?
A. *Your cheeks are like peaches – football peaches.*

Q. What did the girl say to her boyfriend?
A. *Your teeth are like stars – they come out at night.*

Q. What else?
A. *You remind me of the sea – you make me sick!*

Q. What else?
A. *Your lips are like petals – bicycle pedals.*

Q. What did two raindrops say to a third?
A. *Two's company, three's a cloud.*

Overheard:　'Will you love me when I'm old
　　　　　　and grey?'
　　　　　　'Of course I do, darling!'

Q. What did the puddle say to the rain?
A. *Drop in some time.*

Q. Why did he call her 'Honey'?
A. *Because she had a comb in her hair!*

Q. What did the bald
　 man say to his comb?
A. *I'll never part from you.*

SHE LOVES ME,
SHE LOVES ME NOT . . . .

Q. What do squirrels give each other on Valentine's Day?
A. *Forget-me-nuts.*

Q. What's grey and white and red all over?
A. *A bashful elephant in love.*

Q. How do elephants find each other in the dark?
A. *Delightful!*

Patient: Can a man fall in love with an elephant?

Doctor: Of course not!

Patient: Well, do you know anyone who wants to buy a large engagement ring?

Q. What sound do hedgehogs make when they kiss?
A. *Ouch!*

Q. Why did the hedgehog cross the road?
A. *To show his girlfriend he had guts. (Ugh!)*

Q. How do porcupines kiss?
A. *Very carefully!*

Q. How do mice kiss?
A. *Mouse-to-mouse.*

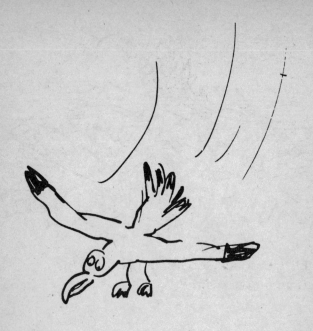

Q. What's the most romantic part of the sea?
A. *The place where buoy meets gull.*

Q. How does a boat show its affection?
A. *It hugs the shore.*

Q. Why don't wood-peckers have girlfriends?
A. *Because they're always boring.*

Q. When is a ship in love?
A. *When it's attached to a buoy.*

Q. What goes 'chuff-chuff' at a wedding?
A. *The bride's train.*

Q. How does the ocean date?
A. *It goes out with the tide.*

Q. Why was Frankenstein never lonely?
A. *He was good at making friends.*

Q. Why was Frankenstein's monster unhappy?
A. *Because he broke up with his girlfriend.*

Q. Why did the girlfriend of Frankenstein's monster break off with him?
A. *Because he had a crush on her.*

Did you hear about the two vampires? They loved in vein.

Q. Why don't vampires get kissed much?
A. *They have bat breath.*

Q. Who did the vampire marry?
A. *The girl necks door.*

Q. Why was the ghost lonely?
A. *Because he had no body to go out with.*

Q. What kind of girl does a mummy go out with?
A. *Any girl he can dig up.*

Q. Why did the banana go out with a prune?
A. *It couldn't get a date.*

Q. Why don't bananas get lonely?
A. *They go around in bunches.*

Q. Why did the orange cry?
A. *It went out with an onion.*

Q. How can you tell a boy-moose from a girl-moose?

A. *By his moose-tache.*

Q. Why did the girl put sugar under her pillow?

A. *She wanted sweet dreams.*

Q. What happened when a couple tried to kiss each other in the dense fog?
A. *They mist.*

Q. Did you hear about the couple who met in a revolving door?
A. *They've been going round together ever since.*

Did you hear about the two Martians who landed on Earth and who both fell in love with the same traffic light?
'I saw her first,' protested one.
'So what?' said the other. 'I'm the one she winked at.'

Two Martians landed near a large town.
Pointing to the TV aerials, one said to the other with a grin:
'Look at all those lovely girls!'

Q. What would the boy have who gave five chocolates to Sally, and five to Karen?

A. *Two new girlfriends.*

Q. Why are cricketers Romeos?
A. *Because they bowl a maiden over.*

Did you hear about the schoolboy who thought his teacher loved him? She kept putting Xs by his sums . . .

Did you hear about the unlucky princess? She kissed a handsome prince and he turned into a frog . . .

Did you hear about the cockerel who fell in love with the hen? She egged him on . . .

Did you hear about the snake who fell in love with his other end?

Q. How do you send a love letter to a Viking?
A. *By Norse Code.*

Q. What happened when the Eskimo fell out with his girfriend?
A. *He gave her the cold shoulder.*

Q. Who was the first person to swear?
A. *Eve: when Adam asked if he could kiss her, she said, 'I don't care Adam if you do.'*

Q. Did Adam and Eve ever have a date?
A. *No, they had an apple.*

HAPPY EVER AFTER . . . ?

Did you hear about the girl who was engaged to a man with a wooden leg? Her father broke it off.

Q. Why is an engaged girl like a telephone?
A. *They both have rings.*

Q. What did the big telephone say to the little telephone?
A. *You're too young to get engaged.*

Q. Why didn't Dracula get married?
A. *Because he was a bat-chelor.*

Q. What's the difference between a married
man and a bachelor?
A. *One kisses his missus, the other misses his
kisses.*

Q. Why did the ant elope?
A. *Nobody gnu.*

Q. Who can marry a lot of girls and still be
single?
A. *The minister.*

Q. Why is the bride unlucky on her wedding-day?
A. *Because she never marries the best man.*

Q. Did you hear about the couple who lived in a lighthouse?
A. *They say their marriage is on the rocks.*

Q. Why did the school-teacher marry the caretaker?
A. *Because he swept her off her feet.*

Q. What is the ultimate?
A. *The last person you'd marry.*

Q. What do you call spiders on their wedding day?
A. *Newly-webs.*

Overheard: 'My wife treats me as a god: she keeps giving me burnt offerings.'

Did you hear about the two elephants who got engaged? They planned a mammoth wedding . . .

Roo loves Pooh

Cinderella married for mon
(she really put her foot in it

Eve
was
framed

If MUSIC BE   give her
THE Food of   something
love I need   nice this
retuning   weekend~
                     YOUR PAY
                     PACKE

I love mankind.

it's people I cant stand.

Say it with
flowers.
give him
a triffid.

I love GRILS
dont you mean girls?
hat about us GRILS, then?

Flower
power
rules - bouquet

You have to kiss
a lot of toads
before you find
your prince!

Is there
life after marriage?

EVERY TIME
I SEE HIM
MY KNEES
TURN TO JELLY
Is it love or
Is it fear?

MARRIAGE
is like a
bed of ROSES -
- look out
for the thorns